Mummy's a Soldier

Mummy's a Soldier

Copyright © 2024 by Angel Pie Publishing

All rights reserved.

No part of this publication may be reproduced, distributed, or transmitted in any form or by any means, including photocopying, recording, or other electronic or mechanical methods, without the prior written permission of the publisher, except as permitted by U.K. copyright law. For permission requests, contact Angel Pie Publishing via *TalulaGrey.com.*

The story, all names, characters, and incidents portrayed in this production are fictitious. No identification with actual persons (living or deceased), places, buildings, and products is intended or should be inferred.

ISBN: 978-1-0685078-6-1

This book belongs to...

How to Enjoy This Story

This book is written in a free-form style, without strict rhyme or rhythm, to reflect real-life experiences. Each page explores a different role within the Army, helping children understand why these jobs matter, why helping others is so important, and why sometimes parents must be far from home.

The story is designed to grow with your child, sparking conversations about family, bravery, and the many important roles in the Army. Here are some tips on how to make the most of it with children of different ages.

For Children Under 3

- Explore Together: Focus on the illustrations, describing what you see. Point out people, uniforms, equipment, and places in simple terms.
- Story Moments: Share short phrases like, "Mummy helps keep people safe," or "These soldiers help people in need." Let your child point to things they notice or find interesting.

For Children 3-5 Years Old
•	Read Aloud: Read the story aloud, pausing to explain words and ideas. Use the pictures to help explain terms like "mission," "training," or "international."
•	Encourage Curiosity: Ask questions like, "What do you think Mommy/Daddy does when s/he's away?" or "Who do you think Mummy/Daddy is helping?" This encourages understanding through conversation.

For Children 6 and Older
•	Encourage Reading Together: Invite your child to read along with you or try reading parts on their own. Let them explore the illustrations to discover Army roles and missions.
•	Discuss and Share: Talk about the different roles in the Army and why they're important. You might say, "Mummy/Daddy helps protect people," or "This is a special job that brings peace." Let your child ask questions, and use the book as a way to discuss your family's connection to the Army and the importance of helping others.

This book is an invitation to explore, imagine, and connect. Each page introduces a new role in the Army and tells part of the story of helping others, serving the country, and acting with honour. Through their own sacrifice of having a parent away, military children, too, serve with honour and courage.

However you use it, I hope this story becomes a treasured part of your child's understanding of the Army, the value of service, and the important role their family plays.

My mummy's gone away, to serve overseas.
She is a proud soldier in the British Army.
She is on an important operation,
to support our allies and protect our nation.
Her boots tread lands across the globe,
Promoting peace, liberty, and hope.

My mummy's a hero, in a uniform of green.
Her boots are so polished, they shine, and they gleam.
The boots help her march over mountains so high,
Trek through jungles, or across deserts so dry.
Her uniform protects her in all kinds of weather.
Come rain or shine, her unit stands together.

On her back she carries a Bergen that holds,
All she needs while she's out on patrol.
Including essentials like food and water.
She even carries a stove with fuel and a lighter.
There's a Poncho for shelter with bungees and pegs,
And a sleeping bag for when it's time for bed.

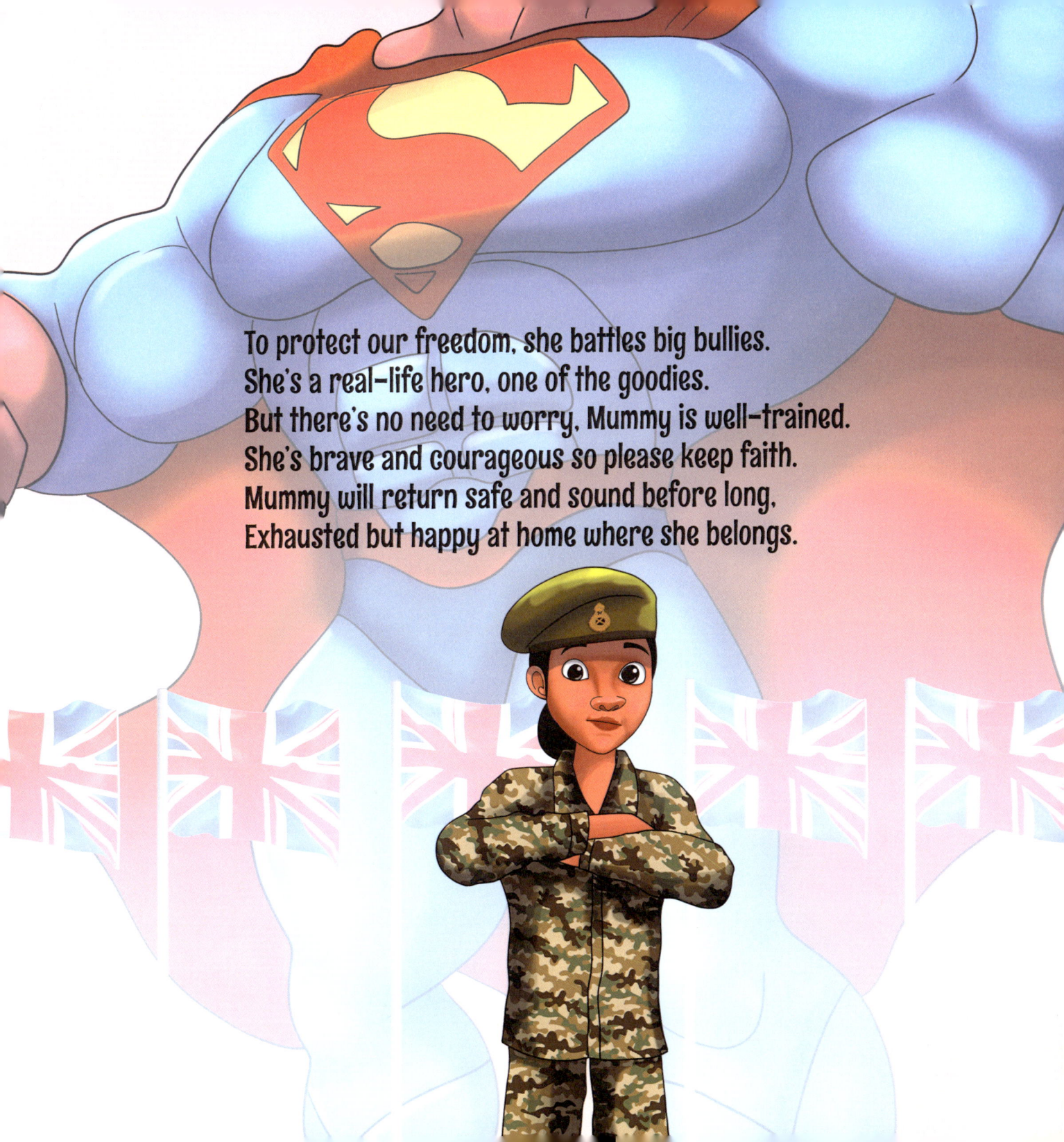

To protect our freedom, she battles big bullies.
She's a real-life hero, one of the goodies.
But there's no need to worry, Mummy is well-trained.
She's brave and courageous so please keep faith.
Mummy will return safe and sound before long,
Exhausted but happy at home where she belongs.

My mummy works with international forces,
To promote global peace, reinforcing
Ties between countries for humanity's sake,
And learning different cultures for unity's sake.
The British Army provides training to other nations,
Fostering peace for future generations.

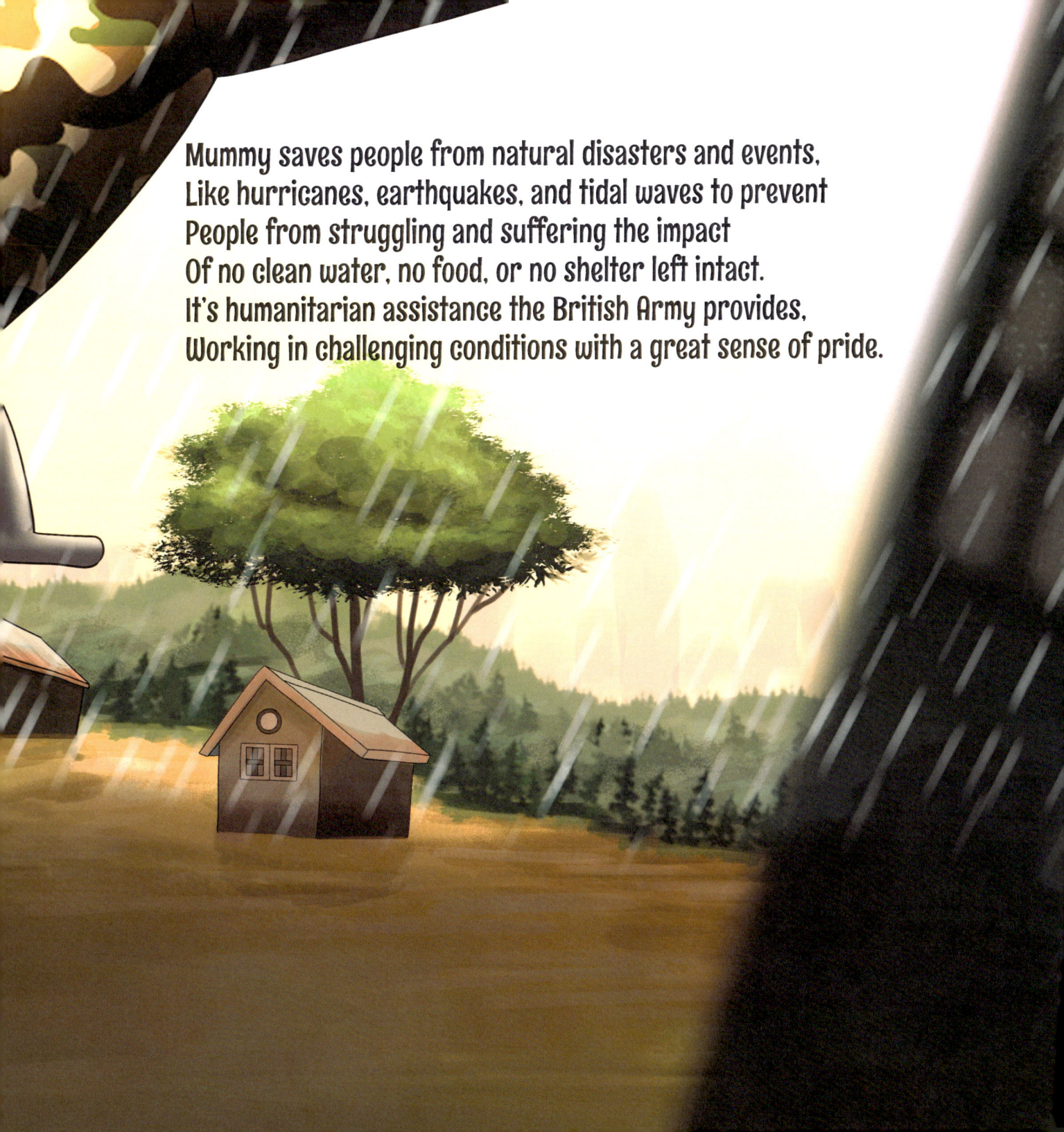

Mummy saves people from natural disasters and events,
Like hurricanes, earthquakes, and tidal waves to prevent
People from struggling and suffering the impact
Of no clean water, no food, or no shelter left intact.
It's humanitarian assistance the British Army provides,
Working in challenging conditions with a great sense of pride.

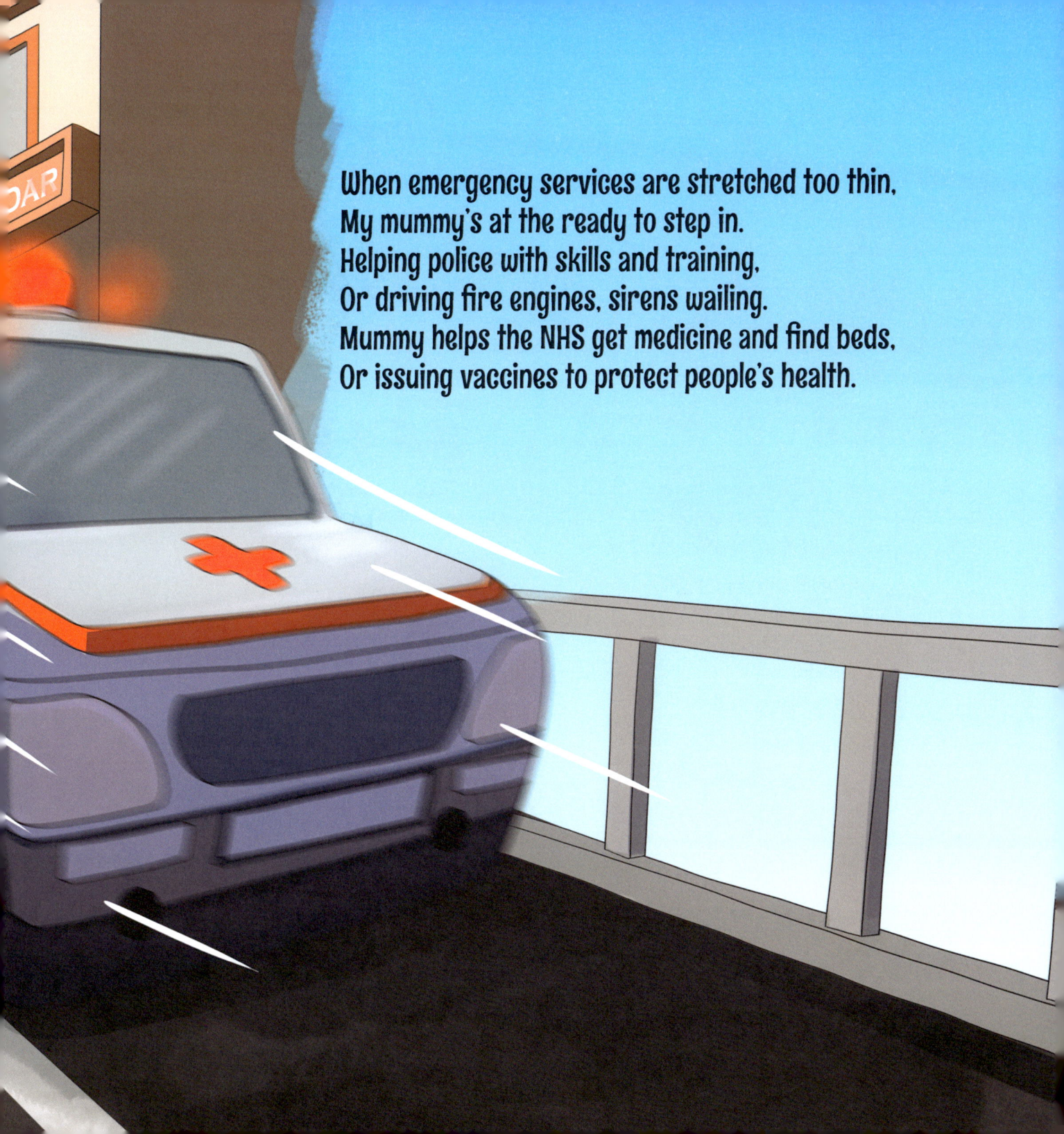

When emergency services are stretched too thin,
My mummy's at the ready to step in.
Helping police with skills and training,
Or driving fire engines, sirens wailing.
Mummy helps the NHS get medicine and find beds,
Or issuing vaccines to protect people's health.

Supporting African nations, where the wild creatures roam,
The British Army has found a new home.
Mummy trains park rangers to patrol and track,
To keep animals safe from being under attack.
Saving elephants, tigers, and rhinos from extinction,
The British Army protecting wildlife is a noble mission.

My mummy's a hero, she builds bridges of peace.
Her presence alone can make conflict decrease.
Her boots march with a powerful force,
Letting other countries know, we're on a peaceful course.
More than just a soldier in a uniform of green,
My mummy is a peacekeeping machine.

There's no need to worry about Mummy feeling lonely.
She's got friends in her unit and her accommodation feels quite homely,
With pictures of me and our family on her wall,
She lays in her bunk at night and thinks of us all.
There are shops and restaurants on the base.
There's even Wi-Fi, so we can chat face-to-face.

Our family gets sad, doing things without Mum is a struggle,
But I help with chores and give lots of cuddles.
We all miss Mummy but have friends who understand.
They're army families too and are around to lend a hand.
There are other children in the same situation.
They miss their parent too, who are away on operation.

I find it so hard when Mummy's away.
I miss her so much and count down the days.
On my wall is a chart for me to tick,
Each day as it passes, hoping it's quick.
Waiting for Mummy to complete her mission and then
Return home to us, safe and sound again.

I have a sweet jar and each sweet represents,
Each day Mummy is away from the day she first went.
Every day I take one sweet savouring its taste.
But for me, it's much sweeter because it's another day faced.
When the day comes that the sweet jar is empty,
I know Mummy's coming home, there'll be celebrations aplenty.

When the sweet jar is empty and the wall chart is done,
I'll be so excited because my mummy's on her way home.
Although I miss Mummy, each day she's gone is rough.
Just like my mummy, I'm brave when the going gets tough.
But one thing's for sure, I'm proud as can be,
To have a mummy who's a soldier in the British Army.

Talula Grey

Talula Grey is a military wife, business owner, and writer, but first and foremost, she is a mummy to her young son, a dog, a cat, and some fish. Talula has been married to her sailor husband for 8 years and enjoys military life; the lows are challenging, but they make the highs so much more exciting.

My Mummy is a Soldier is the third book in the Military Children's Support Series. The other books are 'Daddy's at Sea', 'Mummy's at Sea', 'My Daddy is an Aviator' and 'My Mummy is an Aviator'. Talula is passionate about supporting military children as they make the biggest sacrifices of all.

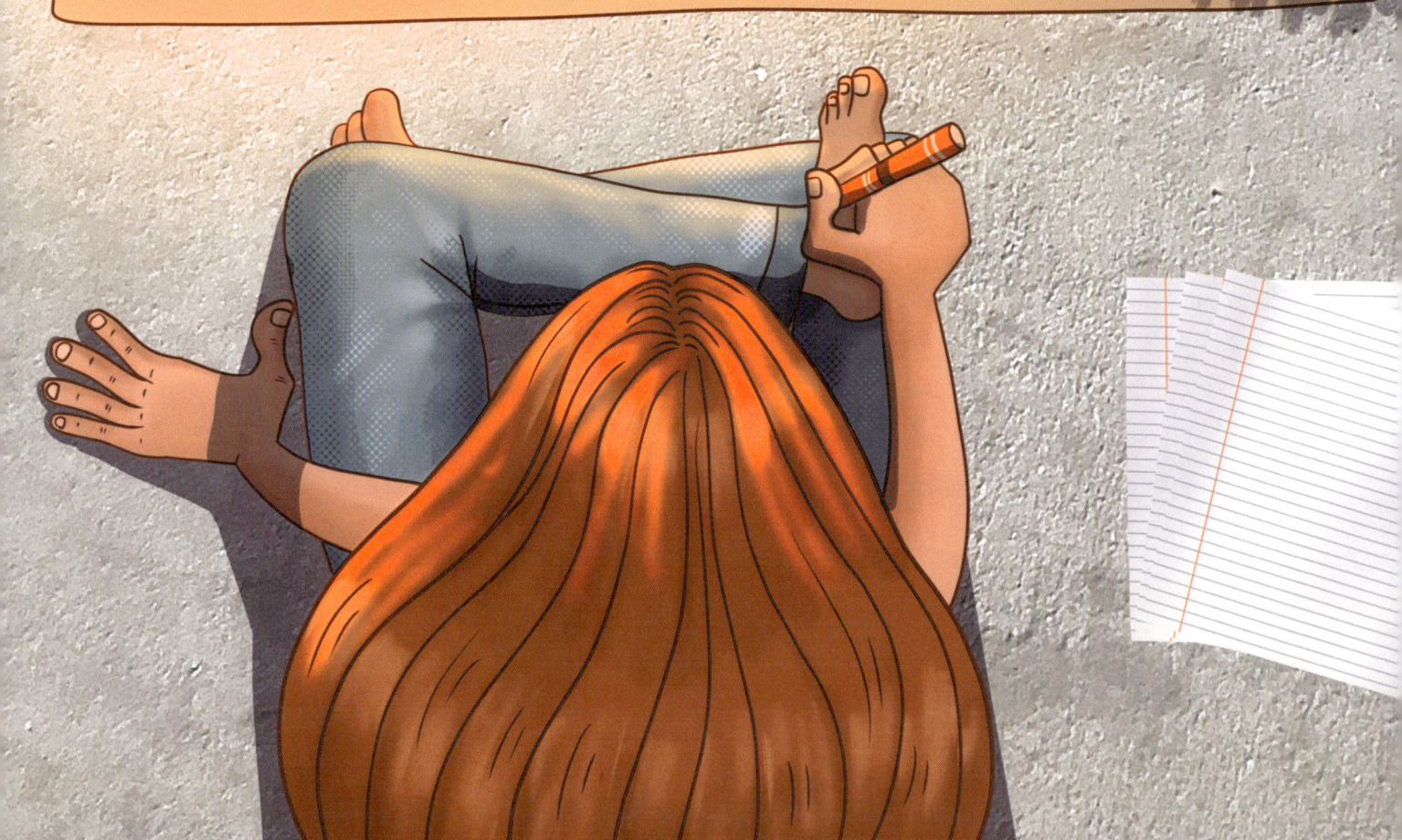

www.ingramcontent.com/pod-product-compliance
Lightning Source LLC
Chambersburg PA
CBRC090838010526
44118CB00007B/240